Changes
Toys and Games

by Liz Gogerly

HODDER
Wayland

an imprint of Hodder Children's Books

Text copyright © 2002 Hodder Wayland

Project manager: Liz Gogerly
Designer: Peta Morey
Picture Research: Shelley Noronha at Glass Onion Pictures
Consultant: Norah Granger

Published in 2002 by Hodder Wayland, an imprint of
Hodder Children's Books
Reprinted in 2003

British Library Cataloguing in Publication Data
Gogerly, Liz
Toys and games. - (Changes ; 2)
1. Toys - Great Britain - History - 19th century - Juvenile literature
2. Toys - Great Britain - History - 20th century - Juvenile literature
3. Games - Great Britain - History - 19th century - Juvenile literature
4. Games - Great Britain - History - 20th century - Juvenile literature
I.Title
790.1'33'0941'09034

ISBN 0 7502 3972 7

Printed in
Hong Kong by Wing King Tong

Hodder Children's Books
A division of Hodder Headline Limited
338 Euston Road, London NW1 3BH

PICTURE ACKNOWLEDGEMENTS:
The publisher would like to thank the following for allowing their
pictures to be used in this publication:
Corbis 7 (top and bottom); Dr Barnardos (cover), 19 (bottom) ; Mary Evans
11 (top), 19 (top right); Hodder Wayland Picture Library/ Huriaha 18 (bottom); Billie Love 16 (top); National Trust 4 (top); Norfolk Museum Services 8
(top), 10 (top), 12 (top), 18 (top); Robert Opie 11 (bottom), 13 (left), 17
(top left); Photodisc (cover); Photofusion/ Bob Watkins 15 (bottom);
Popperfoto 5 (bottom); Science and Society/ Daily Herald Archive 9 (top);
Topham Picturepoint (title page), 5 (top), 6 (top), 9 (bottom), 13 (right), 14
(top), 15 (top), 17 (top right); Zul Mukhida 4 (bottom), 6 (bottom), 8
(bottom), 10 (bottom), 12 (bottom), 14 (bottom), 16 (bottom)

With special thanks to Gamleys toy shop of Brighton for kind permission to
borrow toys for photography purposes.

Contents

Outdoor Games

In the past children often played in the street because there was not enough room at home. They played games like **leap-frog** and **chase**. They had simple toys for outdoors like yo-yos, marbles and balls. Today, we play many of the same games.

In **Victorian** times children often played with hoops. A hoop was pushed along with a stick. It would get faster and faster. The children chased it until it fell down. Then they would start again.

These children from the 1920s are playing a skipping game. They sang a **rhyme** as they skipped. If they tripped on the skipping rope then they were 'out'.

These children from the 1940s are playing hopscotch. It is easy to play. Do you know the rules for this game?

Games that make you Think

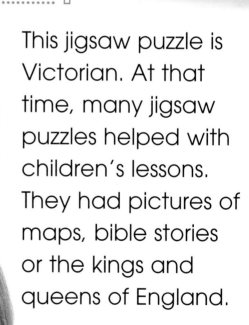

Computer and **electronic** games started to appear in the 1970s. These games are fun and sometimes they help children learn to spell and count. People in the past also knew that the best way to learn is while you are having fun.

This jigsaw puzzle is Victorian. At that time, many jigsaw puzzles helped with children's lessons. They had pictures of maps, bible stories or the kings and queens of England.

These children from the 1920s are enjoying a game of **draughts** outdoors. They need to think carefully if they want to win this board game.

This family is playing Scrabble. Letters are picked out of a bag and used to make words on a board. You need to be lucky and good with words to win.

Games to Win!

Part of the fun of playing games is trying to be the winner. In games like Hungry Hippos you need to be fast to win. In games like Snakes and Ladders you need to be lucky when you roll the dice. Games like these have always been **popular**.

This game is called Picture Lotto. It is from 1910. Lotto is played like **bingo**. Players must cover all the pictures on their card to win the game.

These children are enjoying a game of **bagatelle**. Each player must strike the marbles into the holes on the board to score points.

Here is an electric car-racing game from the 1960s. The idea of this game is to be the fastest car around the track.

Toys you can Build

Children enjoy making models of buildings, cars or even animals. In **Victorian** times wooden building blocks were used to make tall towers or houses. Lego was invented in 1958 and has been **popular** ever since. These little plastic pieces can be made into almost anything you like.

Some blocks were made from stone. These blocks from the 1920s came in different sizes, colours and shapes. Children could copy the pictures of buildings from a book.

These children from the 1930s are playing with **Plasticine**. They are making models of an elephant and a bear.

Airfix models were invented in 1953. Plastic pieces are glued together to make models of aeroplanes or boats. This model is of a ship called the *Mayflower*.

Dolls

Dolls are one of the oldest toys. The first dolls were made from wood. In **Victorian** times dolls were made in factories. Wood, **papier mâché**, cloth or china were used to make these dolls. Most dolls today are made from plastic. Dolls like Barbie and her friend Christie have lots of clothes.

Victorian children from richer homes often had **china** dolls. The dolls' clothes were often made at home. Would you like a doll like these?

This shop from the 1950s has all kinds of plastic dolls. Some dolls have hair that can be washed. Others have eyes that open and shut.

In the 1960s this Action Man doll could be dressed as a soldier. His arms and legs had **joints**. He could be moved into lots of **positions**.

Teddy Bears and other Friends

The teddy bear is quite an old toy. The first teddy was made in the USA in 1903. It was named after the American **president**, Teddy Roosevelt. Today there are all kinds of stuffed toys. This dog **whines** when you squeeze his belly.

These little girls from the 1940s are watching a teddy bears' picnic. Old bears like these were often made from brown fur. They were stuffed with **wood shavings** or straw.

Children loved their teddy bears. Soon other animals were made into stuffed toys too. This girl in the 1950s is cuddling toy animals. Do you know what animals they are?

By the 1980s teddy bears were made in lots of colours and **designs**. Their fur was usually soft and lovely to cuddle.

Moving Toys

Toys that can move by themselves are exciting. Today we have dolls that walk and talk. We have cars and trains that can zoom along. This cyber-dog can sit or wag its tail. Most toys now need **batteries** to make them work. People in the past found many ways to make their toys move.

This **Victorian** boy is holding his wooden sailing boat. He sailed his boat on a pond or stream. The wind would blow the sail and make the boat float along.

This toy robot from the 1950s was moved by clockwork. The key was used to wind up the clockwork machinery inside the robot. The robot would then start to move slowly along.

This van was made in 1958. It has an electric motor. The little boy moves the van by **radio-control**. He can change the direction or the speed of the van using the **handset**.

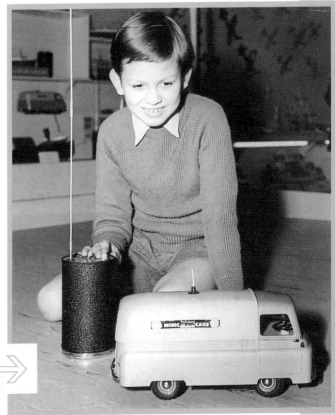

Big Wheels and Bouncy Toys

It is great fun to ride your skateboard or bicycle. You can go as fast as you like. The **Victorians** invented bicycles. Since then we have found lots of ways of whizzing about outdoors.

This **Victorian** wooden horse looks a bit like a scooter. Children could be pushed or pulled along while they sat on the horse.

These children from the 1920s are bouncing on pogo sticks. They jumped up and down until they fell off. Do you have a pogo stick?

In the past many people could not afford to buy toys from a shop. These children have a cart made from old bits of furniture and pram wheels.

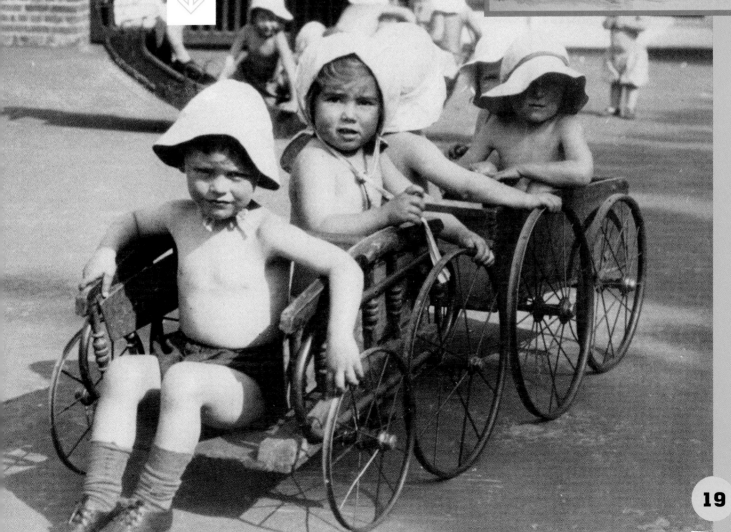

Notes for Parents and Teachers

Changes and the National Curriculum

The books in this series have been chosen so that children can learn more about the way of life of people in the past. Titles such as *A Bite to Eat, Beside the Sea, Dressing Up, Home Sweet Home, School Days* and *Toys and Games* present children with subjects they already know about from their own experiences of life. As such these books may be enjoyed at home or in school, as they satisfy a number of requirements for the Programme of Study for history at Key Stage 1.

These books combine categories from 'Knowledge, skills and understanding' and 'Breadth of study' as required by the National Curriculum. In each spread, the photographs are presented in chronological order. The first photograph is a modern picture that the child should recognize. The following pictures are all historical. Where possible, a wide variety of pictures, including paintings, posters, artefacts and advertisements, have been selected. In this way children can see the different ways in which the past is represented. A lively selection of pictures also helps to develop the children's skills of observation. In turn, this will encourage them to ask questions and discuss their own ideas.

The text is informative and raises questions for the children to talk about in class or at home. It is supported by further information about the historical photographs (see right). Once the children are familiar with the photographs you could ask them to guess when the pictures were taken – if it isn't mentioned in the text. By looking at clues such as clothes, hairstyles, style of buildings and vehicles they might be able to make reasonable guesses. There are further questions to ask your child or class on the right.

About the Photos

Outdoor Games
Pages 4–5

George William Henry Vernon, aged 4, with his wooden hoop at Sudbury Hall in 1858.
Questions to ask:
- What do you think the hoop is made from?
- Do you think this is a little girl or a little boy?

Children playing a game of 'touch' at Blackfriars in London during September 1920.
Questions to ask:
- Do boys play skipping games at your school?
- Do you think the dog is really turning the rope?

Children playing hopscotch in the street – *circa* 1940s.
Question to ask:
- Is this little girl playing properly?

Games that make you Think
Pages 6–7

A Victorian jigsaw puzzle called My Birthday Present.
Questions to ask:
- How many toys can you see in this jigsaw puzzle?
- Can you count the number of pieces in the jigsaw puzzle?

Children from the 1920s playing draughts outdoors.
Questions to ask:
- Do you know another name for the game of draughts?
- What game is played on the same board?

A 1960s family playing Scrabble.
Questions to ask:
- How many people are playing this game?
- Do you know how many letters each player is allowed to hold in a game of Scrabble?

Games to Win!
Pages 8–9

A Victorian lotto set.
Questions to ask:
- Can you name some of the pictures on the cards?
- Do you think you need to be lucky to play this game?

A mother and children playing Coronation Bagatelle in December 1932.
Questions to ask:
- How many marbles can you see on the board?
- Do you think you need to be lucky or good at this game to win?

A young boy trying the latest electrically driven model cars at a toy exhibition in London during November 1961.
Questions to ask:
- How many cars are in the race?
- Is this a game of luck?

Toys you can Build
Pages 10–11

Anchor blocks from the 1920s.
Questions to ask:
- Do you think adults would enjoy this game too?
- What would you build with these blocks?

A trade postcard for Harbutt's Plasticine from early in the twentieth century.
Question to ask:
- How many different colours of Plasticine can you think of?

An Airfix plastic model of the *Mayflower* from the 1950s.
Question to ask:
- What other Airfix models do you know?

Dolls
Pages 12–13

A selection of Victorian dolls.
Questions to ask:
- Do you think the dolls' eyes could move?
- What do you think of the dolls' clothes?

A young girl sitting with a selection of dolls at a trade fair in 1958.
Questions to ask:
- What are these dolls made from?
- Are these dolls like the ones you can buy today?

The first Action Man, which was introduced in 1964.
Questions to ask:
- What are the doll's boots made from?
- How different is this Action Man from the doll you can buy today?

Teddy Bears and other Friends
Pages 14–15

Two sisters watching a teddy bears' picnic in the 1940s.
Questions to ask:
- What do the teddys have around their necks?
- Do you have a teddy like this?

A young girl hugging giant stuffed toys during May 1955.
Question to ask:
- What colours do you think these stuffed toys are?

A young boy playing with a Care Bear, date unknown.
Question to ask:
- Why do you think this teddy bear has a big heart on its stomach?

Moving Toys
Pages 16–17

A young boy holding a toy yacht from 1900.
Questions to ask:
- What uniform is the boy wearing?
- Can you still buy toys like this today?

A Sparky Robot from the 1950s.
Questions to ask:
- What is the robot made from?
- Do you have any clockwork toys?

A young boy demonstrates a radio-controlled Amnivan at a toy fair in London in 1958. At that time the van cost £15.
Questions to ask:
- What is the van made from?
- Do you have a radio-controlled toy?

Big Wheels and Bouncy Toys
Pages 18–19

A wooden horse on wheels from the 1850s.
Questions to ask:
- What is this toy made from?
- Does it look easy to ride?

Swedish children enjoying playing on pogo sticks in 1922. The pogo stick was already popular in France, Britain and the USA.
Question to ask:
- Does jumping on a pogo stick look easy?

Dr Barnados children playing outdoors, date unknown.
Questions to ask:
- How would they have made this cart move?
- How many wheels are there on the cart?

Glossary

bagatelle A game in which small balls or marbles are aimed at holes on a board. Each hole is worth points. Whoever scores the most points wins the game.

battery A small container which stores chemicals that produce electric power.

bingo A game where each player has a card with numbers on it. These numbers can be crossed out when chosen by the caller. The first person to cross out all their numbers is the winner.

chase A running game. One person is usually 'on' or 'it' and chases the other players until he catches one of them. That person is then 'on' or 'it'.

china Thin and delicate pottery that breaks easily. Cups, plates and dishes are often made from china.

designs Different styles and shapes of something.

draughts A board game played by two people. To win the game you capture the other player's pieces.

electronic Describes games or machines which use electricity to make them work.

handset The name of the box you hold in your hand while playing with computer games or radio-controlled toys. It has the buttons and controls for playing the game.

joints The places where bones in the body meet, for example, at the knees, wrists and elbows.

leap-frog A game where players take it in turn to jump with parted legs over others who are bending down.

papier mâché Pieces of paper and glue mixed together, which can be used to make models or pots.

Plasticine A soft plastic dough which can be modelled into any shape.

popular Liked and enjoyed by a lot of people.

positions The different ways a person holds their body – how they sit or stand.

president The person who is in charge of a country.

radio-control To move a toy or object from a distance by radio.

rhyme A short song or poem where the words at the end of a line usually have the same sound as the next line.

Victorian Used to describe anything from the time when Queen Victoria ruled Britain (1837–1901).

whines Makes a long sad sound like crying.

wood shavings Thin slices of wood – almost like pencil shavings.

Further Information

Books to Read
Non-fiction
History From Objects: Toys
(Hodder Wayland, 1996)
Everyday History: Toys and Games by
Philip Steele
(Franklin Watts, 2000)

Fiction
Anna Then, Anna Now by Josette
Blanco and Claude D'Ham
(Young Library, 1989)
The Tale of Two Bad Mice
by Beatrix Potter
(Frederick Warne, 1987)

Sources
Games From an Edwardian Childhood
by Rosaleen Cooper (David and
Charles, 1982)
Teddy Bears by Geneviève and
Gérard Picot (Weidenfield and
Nicolson, 1988)

Websites
www.gold.enta.net/toymuseum.htm
Visit the site for the House on the Hill
Toy Museum and find out more about
your favourite toys.

Website for Teachers
*http://www.educate.org.uk/
teacher_zone/classroom/history/
unit1.htm*
This site suggests activities for studying
the history of toys for pupils at key
stage one.

Museums to Visit
House on the Hill Toy Museum
Stansted, Essex CM24 8SP

Museum of Childhood
42 High Street, Edinburgh EH1

The Bear Museum
38 Dragon Street, Petersfield,
Hampshire GU31 4JJ

The National Museum of Childhood
Cambridge Heath Road, London
E2 9PA

Index